MICROSOFT TEAMS

FOR BEGINNERS 2020

A Dummy to Expert Guide to Collaboration and Communication with Microsoft Teams for Web-Based Meetings, Online Learning, and Administrations

JAMES JORDAN

Legal Notice

CONTENTS

PREFACE

As we journey into this book, you will be learning how to make use of Microsoft Teams application. Guess what? You don't have to be a computer guru to be able to use this application. All you need is to be able to read and write and follow simple instructions. With this ability, you are on your way to exploring Microsoft Teams.

This book is divided into four chapters.

In this first chapter, we will be talking explicitly on Microsoft Teams, i.e. what you need to know about Microsoft Teams. its historical background, meaning, importance to individuals and organizations and the constraints to the use of Microsoft Teams.

The second chapter is focused on basic operations on Microsoft Teams in which we will be talking about the feature of Microsoft teams and how to make use of Microsoft Teams Getting started with Microsoft Teams)

In this same chapter, we will also be taking on how to have chats and conversations, placing voice and video calls, scheduling a meeting, etc.

In the third chapter, our focus will be based on how tips and techniques for the use of Microsoft Teams. Under this, we will be talking about the command bars and keyboard shortcuts used in getting specific tasks done quickly without the needing to go through a long and stressful process.

In the last chapters, we will be discussing some common problems that arise with the use of Microsoft Teams and how to proffer solutions to them. This knowledge will save you the stress of getting frustrated unnecessarily over what you can handle all by yourself with just a simple instruction.

Stay back and enjoy every moment spent exploring this book.

INTRODUCTION

Since the invention of Microsoft by Bill Gates, lots of soft wares have been developed by Microsoft Corporation, and among them is Microsoft Team. Microsoft Team came into existence as an upgrade of Skype for Business, and there lies in some functionalities that can only be found in the Microsoft team. Although Skype for Business is still very much active, Microsoft Team has gone a long way higher than it.

Gone are those days when meetings must be held in a board room where everyone must be in attendance, but with the introduction of Microsoft Teams, this issue has been resolved. Employees don't have to be in the same room together with their colleagues or superiors to get hold meetings or get any task carried out.

Staff who now work remotely has many benefits for businesses, including those who have several locations, large workforces, and departments. They are able to reduce business overheads, thus proving them to be productive throughout the working day, with a low level of stress and boosted morale.

Microsoft teams is a collaboration application or tool that allows team of users in an organization to stay organized and have a conversation all in one places. In this business world today, it is no doubt that Microsoft team have been able to take organizations; both private and public, IT personnel to a higher level through its ability to perform certain functions like having chats and conversation, making of voice and video calls, scheduling of meetings, sharing of files etc.

The features embedded in Microsoft Team make it more interesting to operate and these are features like SharePoint, One Drive, Exchange, Azure Active directory etc.

One interesting thing about Microsoft team is that it contains most of the applications found in Microsoft Office Suite like Excel, Word, PowerPoint, Outlook etc. and it has the capacity to store its data online (cloud computing) without bombarding the computer with large bunk of data. With the way Microsoft teams is configured, it can be accessed on the web, desktop computers and mobile devices.

Microsoft teams are continuously adding new features to improve accessibility and user experience.

In this book, I will be shedding more light on how use Microsoft Team effectively in your organization to achieve your organizational goals and objectives.

CHAPTER ONE

OVERVIEW OF MICROSOFT TEAMS

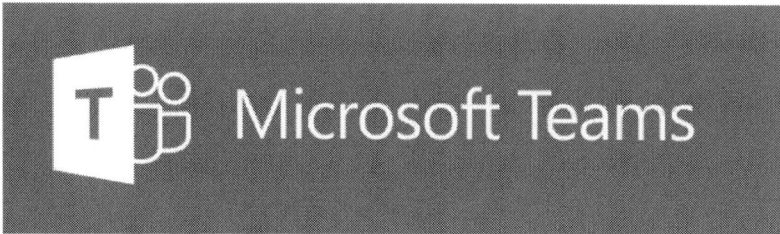

What is Microsoft Team?

This is a collaboration application that allows a team of users to stay organized and have a conversation all in one place. This tool allows for conversation, consistent chat, phone calls, meetings, sharing of files, and application together in one place.

Microsoft teams, inclusive as standard in Microsoft 365 subscriptions is a collaboration tool that allows both office based and remote staff to collaborate with individuals or selected groups of employers or workers within online workspace in Microsoft Team application. Microsoft team allows users to create a team and collaborating through chats (conversation) instead of emails and channels instead of just files.

Microsoft team in its uniqueness can operate vertically all applications made available in Microsoft Office Suite like Excel, PowerPoint, Word, Outlook etc.

Brief History of Microsoft Team

A piece of news broke out that on March 4, 2016, there was a news that Microsoft considered purchasing Slack at the bidding of $8 billion by the then EVP of Application and Service, Mr. Qi Li but Bill Gate the owner of Microsoft corporation was against it saying that the company should focus on improving Skype for Business. After he left that year, Teams was made known to the public as a direct competitor to Slack an application that has almost the same features as Team.

However, Microsoft Team did not allow outside users in and even their users could not switch to other platform and this posed a limitation to the performance of Microsoft Team which was later resolved.

On May 3, 2017, Microsoft announced Microsoft Teams would replace **Microsoft Classroom** in Office 365 Education (formerly known as Office 365 for Education). On September 7, 2017, users of Team began to hear that Skype for Business is now Microsoft and this news was confirmed on September 25, 2017, at Microsoft's annual Ignite conference.

On November 19, 2019, users of Microsoft Teams App were up to 20 million **and there was** an increase of 13 million users as of July. As of March 19, 2020, Microsoft hit 44 million daily users and April 75 million daily users due to the COVID 19 pandemic and it keeps increasing daily.

Importance of Microsoft Teams

It is very important to understand the significance of Microsoft teams; therefore, we will be taking our time to talk about the importance of Microsoft Teams to its users

- **It allows for chats and conversations**: With the use of Microsoft teams, users or members of a team can communicate with each other via chats and conversation. The most interesting part users can check the chat history to refer to any past decisions or actions made and they can always create a private chat for small groups if there is a need for it

- **For making audio and video calls:** Not only cam team members chat via texts, but the Microsoft team also provides a simple and easy-to-use app that allows a person to have a voice conversation or a video meeting with his team.

- **Sharing of files and application**: Microsoft teams allows users to share files and application in the team

- **Creating of workspace**: Microsoft team enables the users to create a workplace that suits the need of the team i.e. the users can create different channels for the team based on their work

- **Clearer project focus**: Microsoft teams allows for focus on a particular project and also helps to manage time better

- **Better communication for enhanced productivity:** With no doubts, Microsoft team has been able to create effective communication channels to its users and this has enhanced productivity in the tasks performed

- **Find location:** With use of Microsoft Team, a user can find the location of a particular place

- **The use Microsoft Office Suite:** With use of Microsoft Team, users can make use of applications made available in Microsoft Office Suite like Word, Excel, PowerPoint, Outlook etc.

- **Command bar and Keyboard shortcuts:** These are special commands or shortcuts that are used to quickly carry out some operations on the Microsoft Team. They help save the stress of going through long processes to get a task performed e.g /command, @command etc.

- **Security:** User login to Microsoft Team using multi factor authentications and secure guest access. With this, there is low tendency of one's account being hacked

- **Customizing the teams' workplace with third party:** Apart from being able to create channels, files, tasks and wikis, Microsoft teams is compatible with different kinds of third party application. With in-built connectors, team can send information to specific team channels using data sources such as Bing News, Facebook pages or Twitter.

- **Real time document collaboration:** team members can collaborate, co-author and edit documents effortlessly at the same time with other users within the organization allowing for effective teamwork.

- **Microsoft Teams is fully integrated:** Microsoft teams is integrated with Microsoft Office 365 with allow users to interact with each other. As a result of the integration, members can calendar, files, notes and attachment among each other. Microsoft Teams is integrated with classic, well-known tools such as Word, Excel, PowerPoint, and some modern tools such as SharePoint, OneNote, and Planner

- **Accessible in all devices**: Microsoft teams can be accessed in all devices; be it on web browser, desktop computers and mobile devices'

- **Built in translator:** Due to diversities in languages, some people are not able to communicate effectively. With the use of Microsoft teams, people can communicate in their different languages without barriers as a result of it having in built translator that helps translate any language.

Constraints to the Use of Microsoft Teams

There is no application in the world no matter how good it is that does not have its shortcomings, therefore, we will be mentioning them below:

- Microsoft teams consume space and data

- In a team, the numbers of channels to be created has limit and this can be a problem to a team if they have exceeded the limit of channels to be created.

- There are too many tools to be used thus, confusing the users

- With poor signal, there could be a disruption in the use of Microsoft teams and this is due to the fact that Microsoft Team run multiple

- There may be difficulty in locating a particular chat if you don't remember where the chat was had

- Importing and exporting of channels, data and files from one team to the other is not possible in Microsoft Team thus, making it one of the limitations to the use of Microsoft Team. In addition, a channel cannot be created separately from a team

- When a team is created, any file or document posted in the team is made available for every member to see, thus there is no room to restricting any member to see what you don't want them to see

- Another constraint to the use of Microsoft team is that, the name of a team can be duplicated twice thus, confusing the users.

- Another threat to the use of Microsoft is that when a user wishes to delete a group, every channel or group created within it will be deleted automatically with the team

Users of Microsoft Teams

Few among the users of Microsoft team will be mentioned below and they are as follows

- ✓ Business organizations

- ✓ IT personnel

- ✓ Schools

- ✓ Online Business

CHAPTER TWO

OPERATIONS ON MICROSOFT TEAMS

The Basic Features of Microsoft Teams

Before we proceed to the various operations that can be carried on Microsoft teams, it is imperative to discuss the basic features of Microsoft teams to have a clearer understanding of how Microsoft teams operate.

Azure Active Directory: This is an essential feature of the Microsoft team that stores identity information of the users, including their password. With this service, users can create an ID that enables them to sign in to teams. It also helps to prevent users against cyberattacks on their accounts.

Exchange Online: This is also an essential feature of Microsoft teams that hosts emails, calendars, and tasks on the PCs, the web, and mobile devices and also grant access to them. With exchange online,

users can save large bunks of emails or data without fear of losing them

Share Point Line: This is the feature that allows for the storing and transferring of files and folder in a team channel. In other words, SharePoint Online allows the users to receive, store, search, track, manage, and utilize digital documents. Without SharePoint online, files, or documents can be shared.

OneDrive for Business: just like SharePoint Online, these features allow users to share files and folders but the difference is just that files and folders shared are in on one chat or private chat.

Office 365 Application: This is the most important feature of the Microsoft team in which all other features like Azure Active Directory, Exchange Online, etc. are dependent on. Right in this application entails Word, Excel, PowerPoint, Outlook, OneNote, etc.

How to Access Microsoft Teams

To make us of Microsoft teams, there are however three clients who can access Microsoft Teams and we will be discussing them briefly as follows:

- **Web client**: Here, Microsoft Teams can be accessed on the internet browser. To use Team effectively, the browser must be configured to accept cookies from third party. To access the Team on the web, the user must input the url address on the browser(https://teams.microsoft.com). Not every browser supports the web client. Thus, these are the following browsers that support web client
    - ✓ Edge 12+
    - ✓ Chrome 51.0
    - ✓ Internet Explorer 11+
    - ✓ Firefox 47.0

- **Desktop client**: The Microsoft Teams app can be accessed on desktop computer with 32- and 64-bit version of windows. The desktop client app can be downloaded and installed directly from https://teams.microsoft.com
- **Mobile Apps**: Microsoft teams can be accessed on Android, IOS(Apple) and Windows devices. To get the app on Android phones, the end user must go to Google Play Store, for IOS(Apple) mobile devices, the user must go to Apple Play Store and for Windows phones, the users must go Microsoft Store on their phones to get the application downloaded and installed.

  The following are the supported versions of mobile devices that are compatible with use of Microsoft Team
    - Android 4.4 or later
    - IOS 10.0 or later
    - Window phone: Window 10 Mobile

How to Create an Account on Microsoft Teams

Here we shall be making use of the application for a step by step procedure to create an account on Microsoft team

- ❖ Search for Microsoft team app on your computer or mobile devices and click on it and the login page below will pop up, then click on sign up for free.

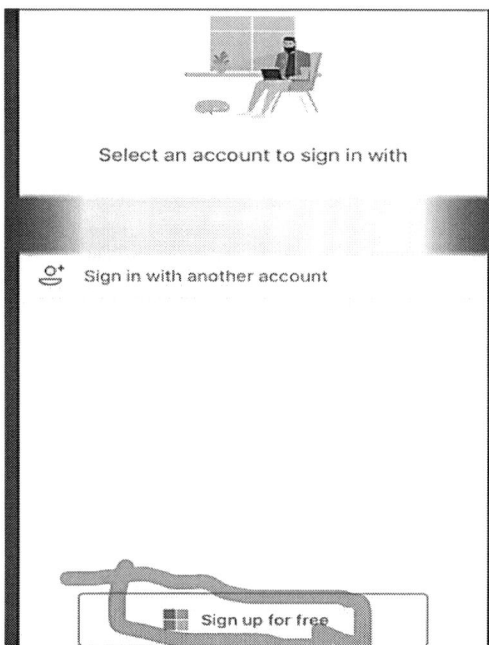

Select an account to sign in with

Sign in with another account

Sign up for free

- put in a valid email account you will like to use for Microsoft Team sign-in account as shown in the picture below

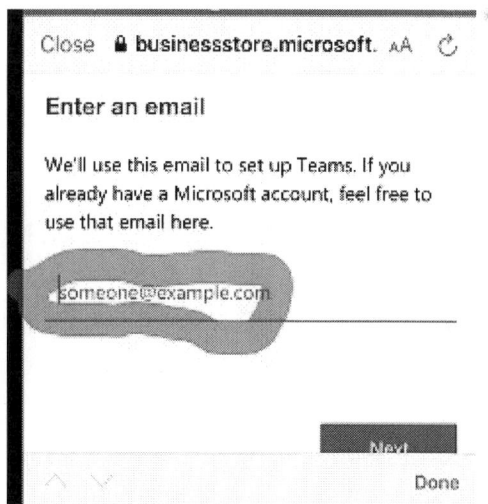

Close 🔒 businessstore.microsoft. ᴀA ↻

Enter an email

We'll use this email to set up Teams. If you already have a Microsoft account, feel free to use that email here.

someone@example.com

Next

Done

- On this page, different kinds of accounts will be displayed in which you have to select the one you wish to open be it for school, friends, and family or work. Chose the one you desire

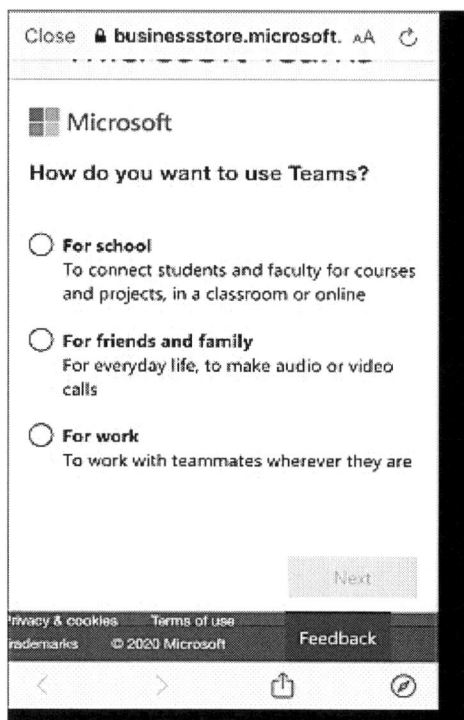

- You will be asked to create an account and where you will be directed to create a password then click on next here on this page.

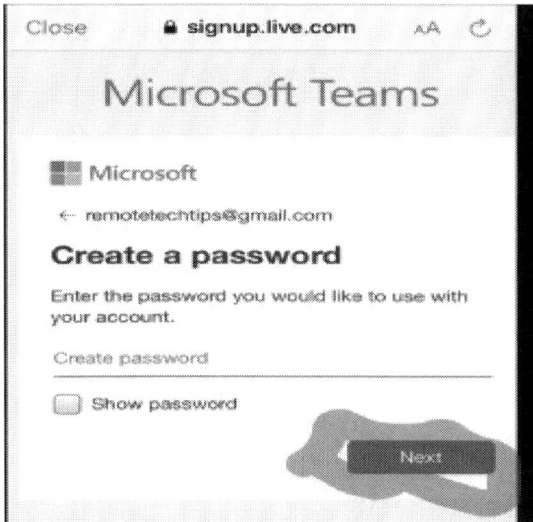

- In this page, a verification code will be sent to your mail that must be Inputted to get the account activated

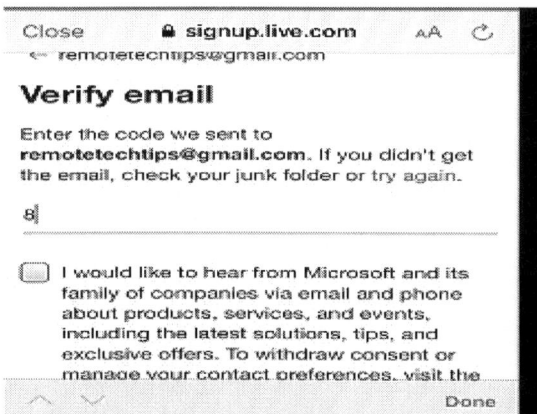

- On this page, your name, company's name and country will be requested for and then click on Set up teams
  Note: Company's name will be requested for when you open Microsoft Teamwork account

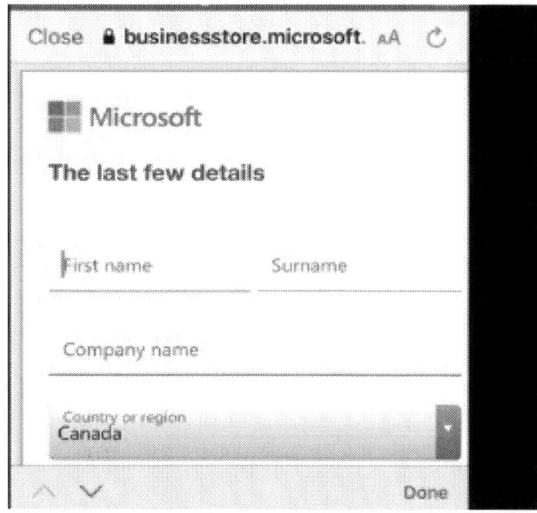

- Here on this page, you will be requested to wait so that your account can be successfully created and activated.

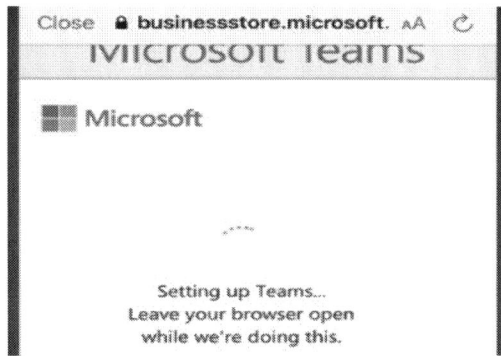

- After following the above steps, you will be told to sign in with your email address and account used while registering. If you have followed the steps as instructed, you are on your way to enjoying Microsoft Teams either on your computer or mobile devices

Sign in using your work or school account.

Sign-in address

Sign in

Get help with signing in

How to create a team on Microsoft Teams

Before creating a team lets quickly talk about what a team is. A team is the main location where a group of people with common work goals can have a persistent conversation, join forces together to

work on projects, and create work products. Without first creating a team,

channels and tabs cannot exist because the Team is where they are located.

Now let's create a team

- The first step to creating a team is open your Microsoft Team app with your account logged in, then click on the "team icon" as shown on the image below

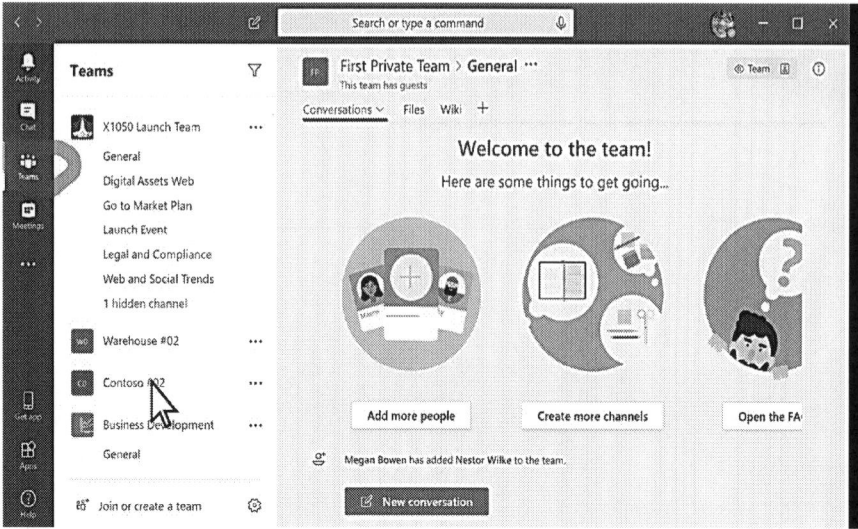

- Then click on "join or create new team" on the lower bottom of the screen

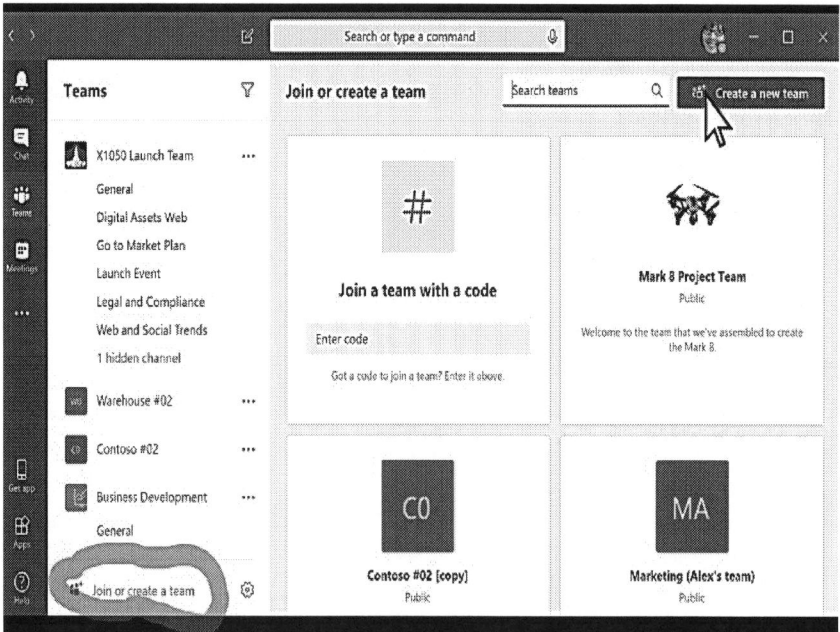

- Click on "Create new team" at the right hand of the screen where you will be asked questions like "Build a team from the scratch or Create from existing group". Choose the one that suits your purpose

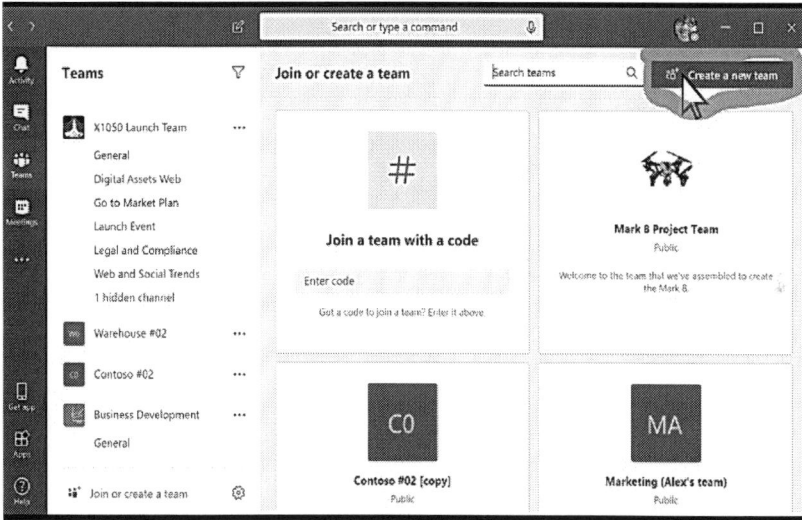

- In the next page, you will be inquired if you intend making the group private, public or org-wide

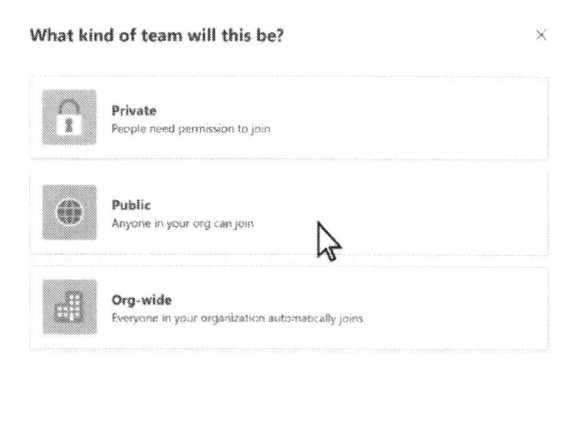

- After you must have followed the above instruction, you will be told to give the team name and the description of the group then click on create

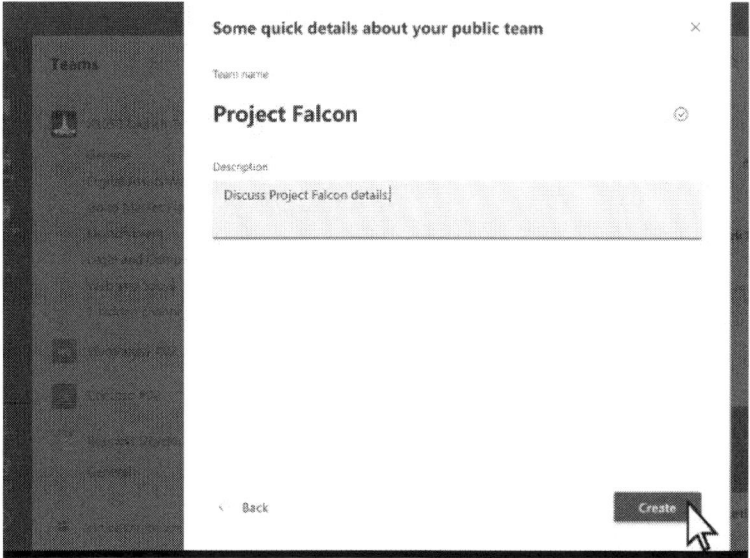

- Immediately you are done creating the group, you can as well add a member to the group and this is shown in the image below

Add members to Project Falcon

Start typing a name, distribution list, or security group to add to your team. You can also add people outside your organization as guests by typing their email addresses.

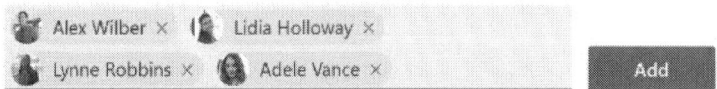

Alex Wilber × | Lidia Holloway ×

Lynne Robbins × Adele Vance ×   Add

Note: Only a team owner can add members

Microsoft Teams Channels

Channels are created within a team to distinguish conversations, chats, and contents for different topics, projects, disciplines, and activities to be carried out on the Team. You can choose to give each channel names that suit its purpose and functionality.

It is important to note that every channel contains three default tabs which are

1. Conversation tab
2. File tabs
3. Wiki tabs

How to Create Channel in Microsoft Teams

Now let's create a channel

- Click on the ellipse button (three dots ...) next to the team name

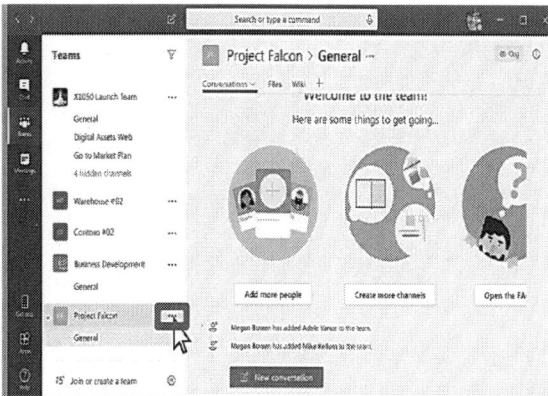

- On this page, click on "Add new channel"

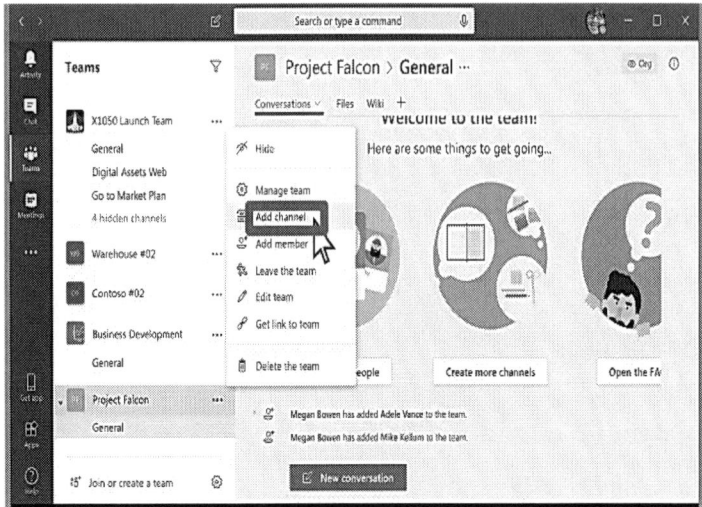

- The next action to take in this page is to name the channel, state the description of the channel and decide if the channel list is to be visible on everyone channel list then click on "add"

Working with Tabs

Tabs are important features located in channels that house content or project connected to a cloud-based service. Three main tabs come with a channel and theses tabs are conversation, files, and wiki tabs. The conversation and file tabs cannot be deleted due to their major functions in making Microsoft Teams work effectively but the Wiki tabs can be deleted. However, other tabs can be created and they are called customized tabs

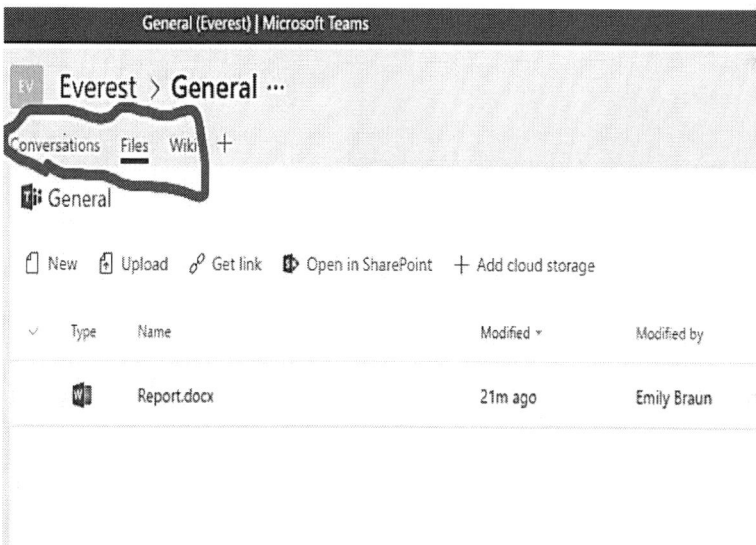

Conversation tabs: This is where an interactive conversation is engaged with your team members. With the conversation tab, you and your team members can use the chat features made available in the conversation tab. To start a message, one needs to enter a message in the conversation box and then send it

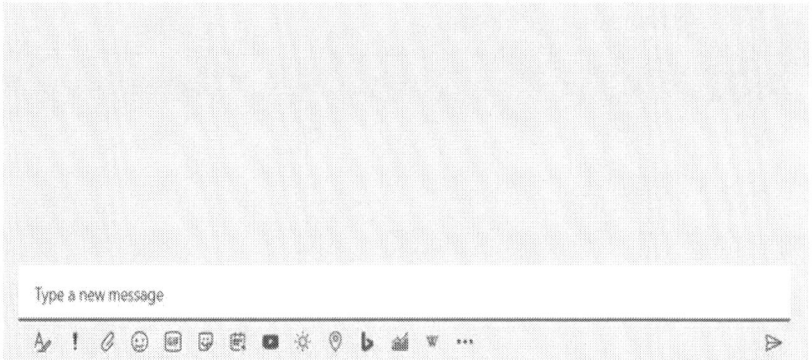

Type a new message

File tab: The File tab is where every document is that is shared and uploaded is found. One can view, upload, and share documents through this tab. All documents found in the file tab are stored in the SharePoint document library

How to Upload Files using the File Tab

- Click on the File tab

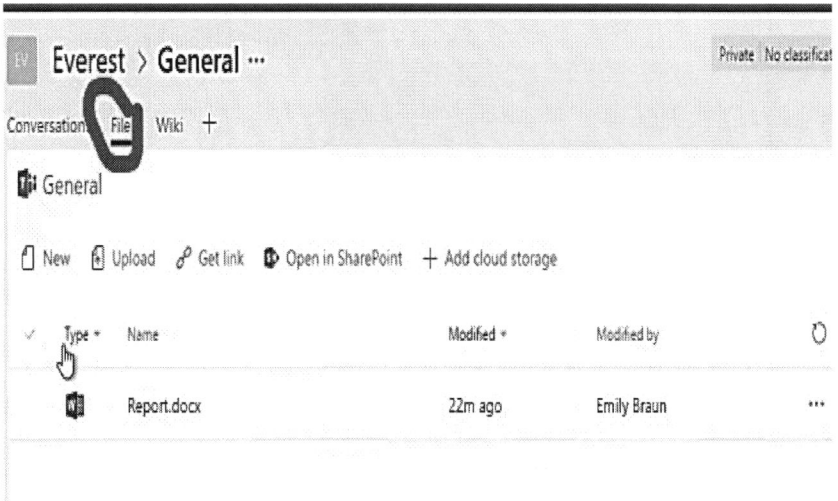

Everest > General ···

Private No classificat

Conversation File Wiki +

General

New   Upload   Get link   Open in SharePoint   + Add cloud storage

Type	Name	Modified	Modified by	
	Report.docx	22m ago	Emily Braun	···

- Then click on upload

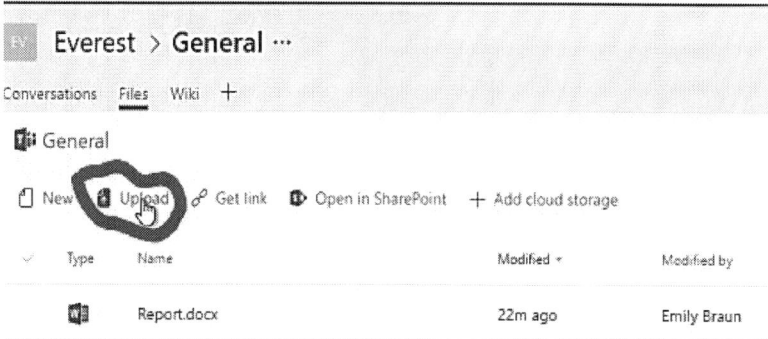

- Select the file to upload

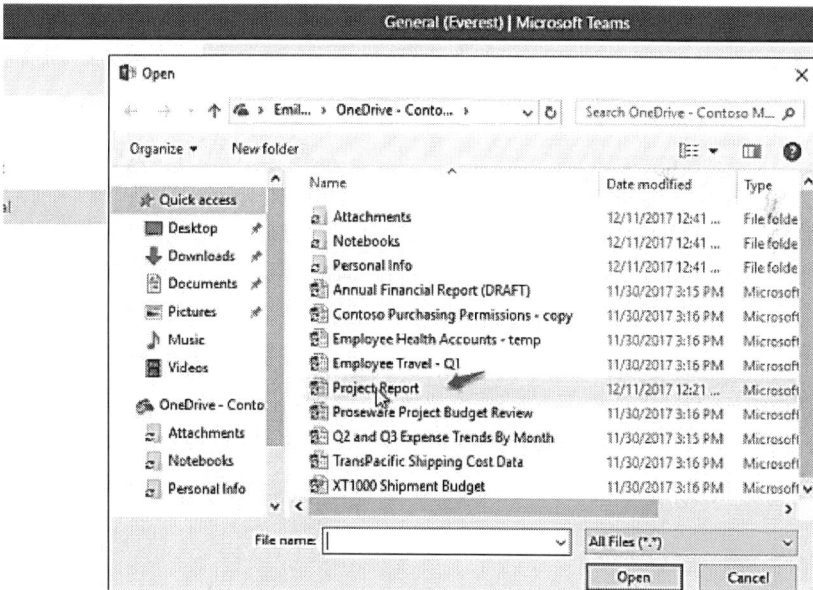

- Then click on open

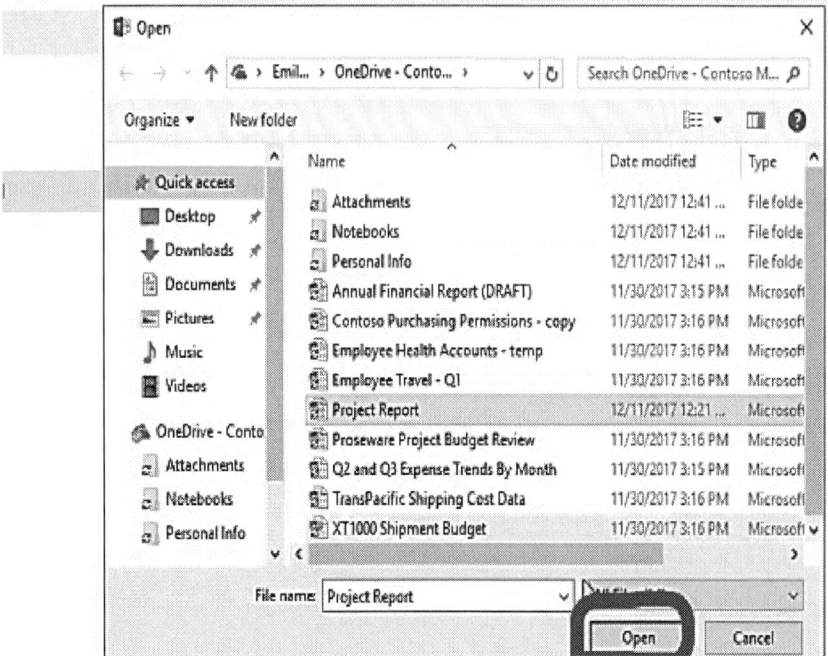

How to Download Files in the File Tab

- Click on the document to be downloaded

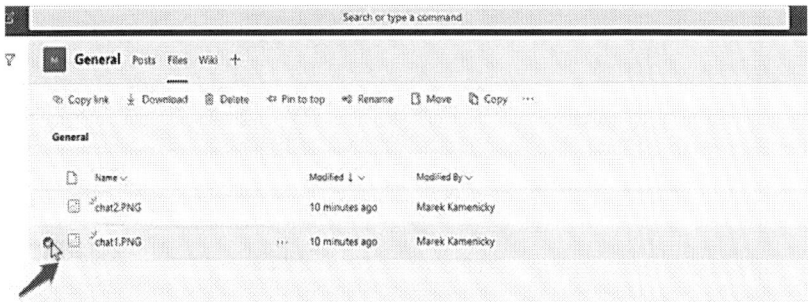

- Click on the download and automatically, the document is downloaded

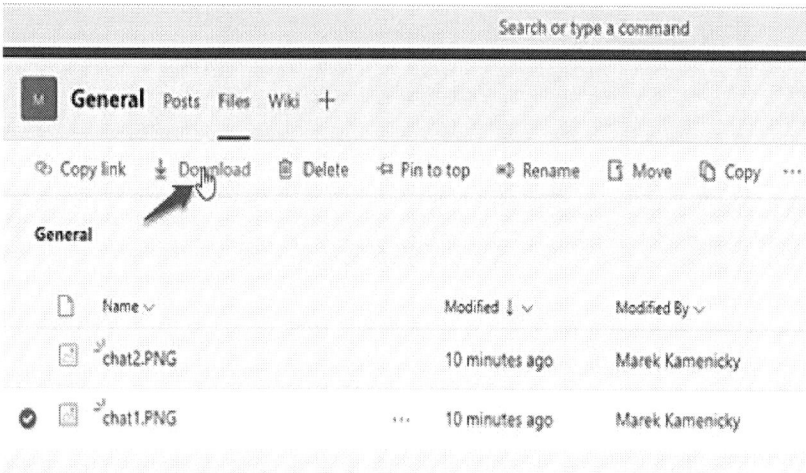

To carry out other modifications like delete, move, download, etc. on a file, follow the procedures

- Click on the file that is highlighted in blue and click on the three dots

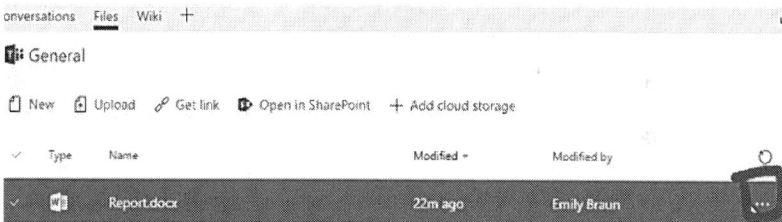

- Click on any action you want to carry out, then click on confirm

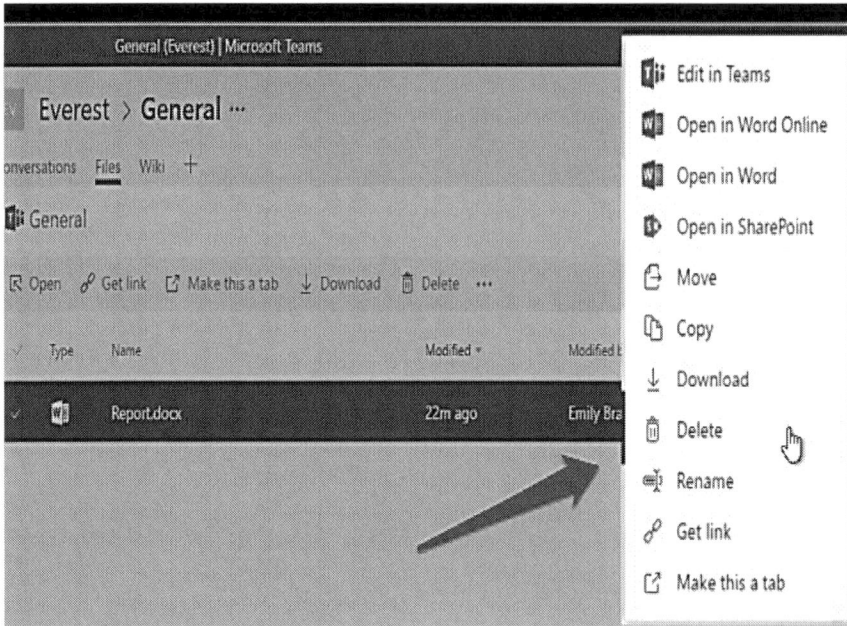

Wiki Tab

This comprises of pages and section with all the usual formatting options such as bold, italics, underlined text, highlighting head and lists. Every document in the wiki tab is called a page and each page contains different sections. The wiki tab is used by the organization to present information in the form of a checklist or steps of a process. The content in a wiki tab like file tab is also stored in the SharePoint site collection

Custom Tabs

Apart from the default tabs; the Conversation, Files and Wiki tabs, Microsoft Team allows you to create your own tabs, and these tabs are called custom tabs. The most common tabs are shown in the picture.

How to Create a Custom Tab

Select the plus (+) icon at the right of your existing tabs

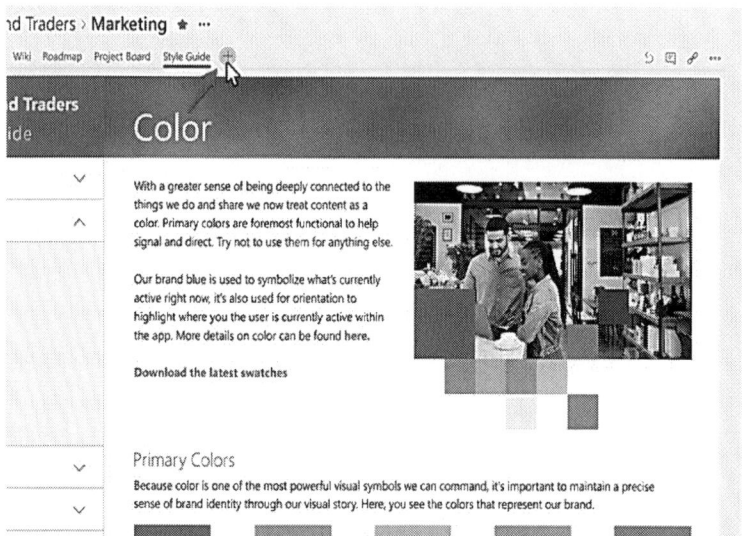

On this page, the custom tabs available will be displayed, click on any

Name the new tab as you want, and then choose one of your
selected workspaces from the drop-down menu.

Add a PowerBI report to your channel. You can even add multiple reports to the same
tab. Find out more.

Tab Name

Workspace

Northwind Traders

Select Report

○ Retail Sales ○ Opportunity Count Overview
○ Opportunities ○ Revenue Analysis
○ Connected Cars ○ Store Sales Overview
○ VSO Status ○ Web Performance Metrics
○ District Monthly Sales ○ Vehicle Health Report
○ July Sales Report ○ July Revenue Analysis

Cancel   Save

Click the Save button.

Add a PowerBI report to your channel. You can even add multiple reports to the same
tab. Find out more.

Tab Name

Site Metrics

Workspace

Northwind Traders

Select Report

○ Retail Sales ○ Opportunity Count Overview
○ Opportunities ○ Revenue Analysis
○ Connected Cars ○ Store Sales Overview
○ VSO Status ● Web Performance Metrics
○ District Monthly Sales ○ Vehicle Health Report
○ July Sales Report ○ July Revenue Analysis

Cancel   Save

Having Chats and Conversation on Microsoft Teams

In chat, you can have one-on-chat or group chat with your teammates. To start chatting, the following steps should be taken

- Click on" chat" at the left-hand side of the screen

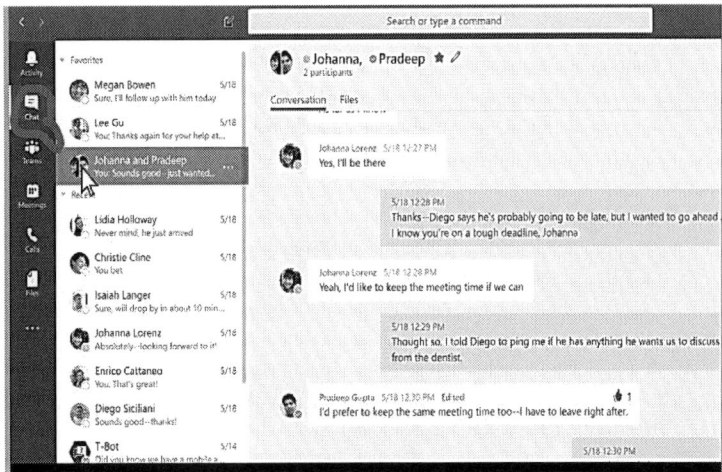

- To begin a new conversation, click on the new chat icon at the top of the screen

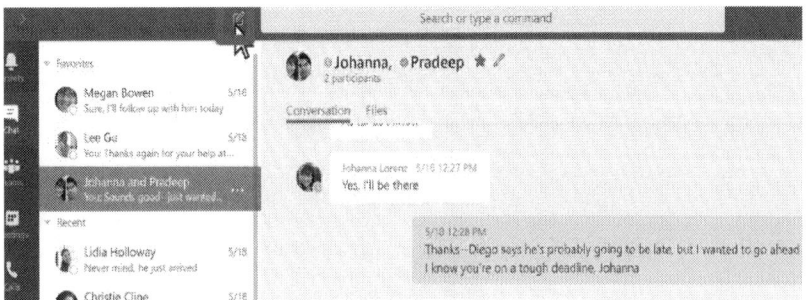

- Type in the column provided the name of the person or group you want to reach out to

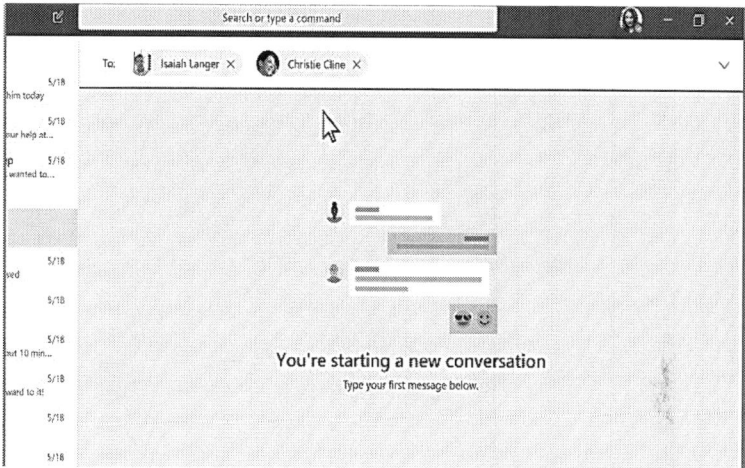

How to Make Voice and Video Call on Microsoft Team

To make a voice call, it is imperative to know that the devices to be used must have a microphone and for the video call, the devices must have a webcam. If your devices possess the following things mentioned, you are on your way to making voice and video calls.

Placing a Voice Call

There may arise instances where there may be no time to create a chat with a team member or the content of the message to be conveyed cannot be well understood through chat. The user can decide to place a call.

Here are few tips to place a call

- Click the chat icon located on the left in the Microsoft Teams app.

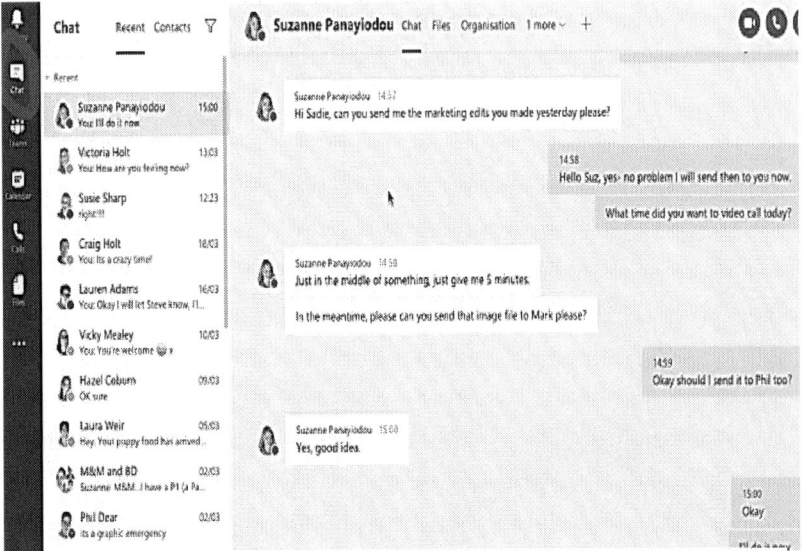

- Select the person you want to call from your recent chat or use the search box to locate them

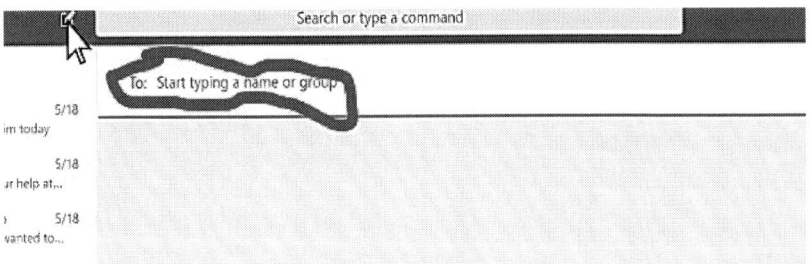

- Click the phone icon situated on the top right of the chat message to place your call

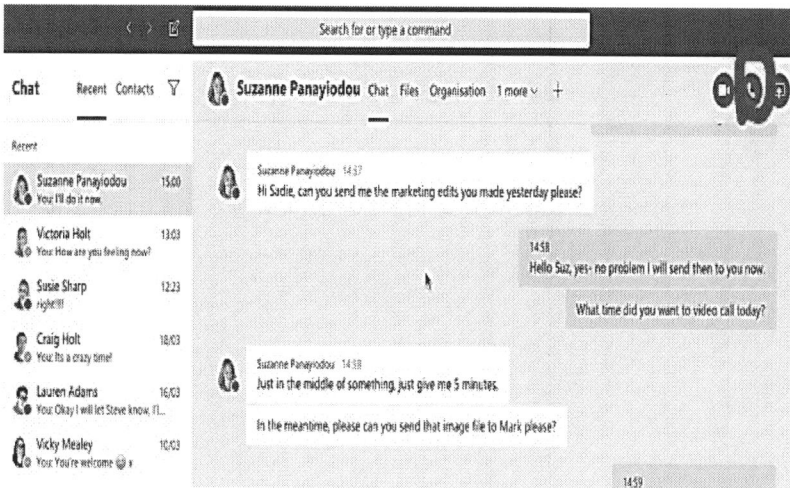

Search for or type a command

Chat   Recent Contacts

Recent

Suzanne Panayiodou 15:00
You: I'll do it now.

Victoria Holt 13:03
You: How are you feeling now?

Susie Sharp 12:23
right!!!

Craig Holt 18:03
You: Its a crazy time!

Lauren Adams 16:03
You: Okay I will let Steve know, I'l...

Vicky Mealey 10:03
You: You're welcome 😊 x

Suzanne Panayiodou Chat Files Organisation 1 more ∨ +

Suzanne Panayiodou 14:37
Hi Sadie, can you send me the marketing edits you made yesterday please?

14:58
Hello Suz, yes- no problem I will send then to you now.

What time did you want to video call today?

Suzanne Panayiodou 14:58
Just in the middle of something, just give me 5 minutes.

In the meantime, please can you send that image file to Mark please?

14:59

- You will then be brought to the call screen as seen below in the image

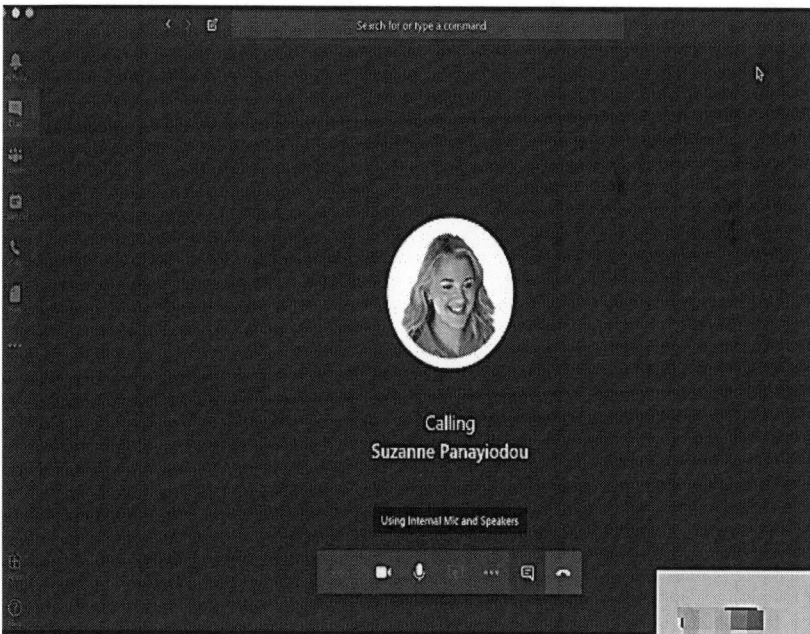

Placing a Video Call

With video calls, you can communicate with your team members face to face even without being together with them. Making video calls is almost the same procedure as making a voice call with just a slight difference.

Now let's make a video call

Click the chat icon located on the left in the Microsoft Teams app.

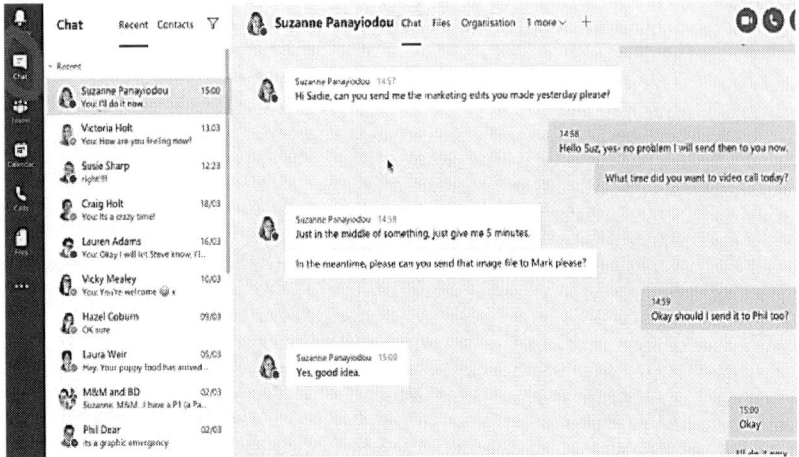

- Select the person you want to make a video call from your recent chat or use the search box to locate them

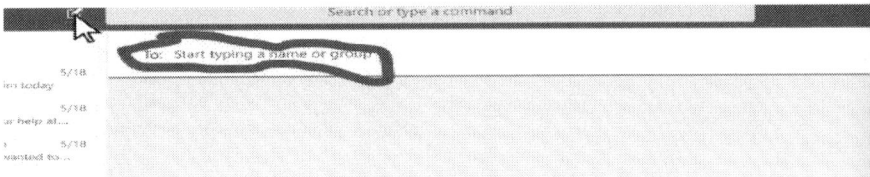

- Click on the phone icon located on the top right of the chat message to place your video call

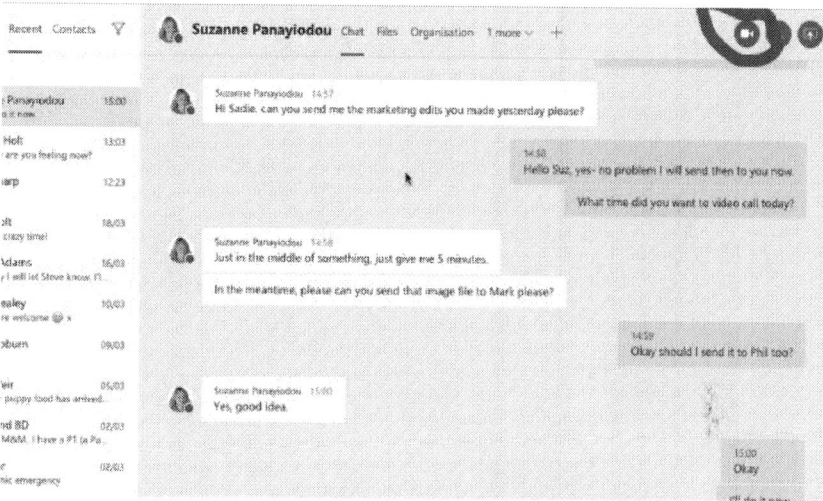

- In this page, the video call screen will be displayed

How to Schedule Meeting on Microsoft Teams

It is no doubt in the business world that money, time and energy wasted on holding meetings are high but guess what? With the use of Microsoft teams, organization in the business world can hold meetings with ease and less time being spent on it.

With following tips that we will be checking out here, I am certain you will be able to schedule a meeting making use of your Microsoft Teams app.

- Click on the calendar on the left of the Team app

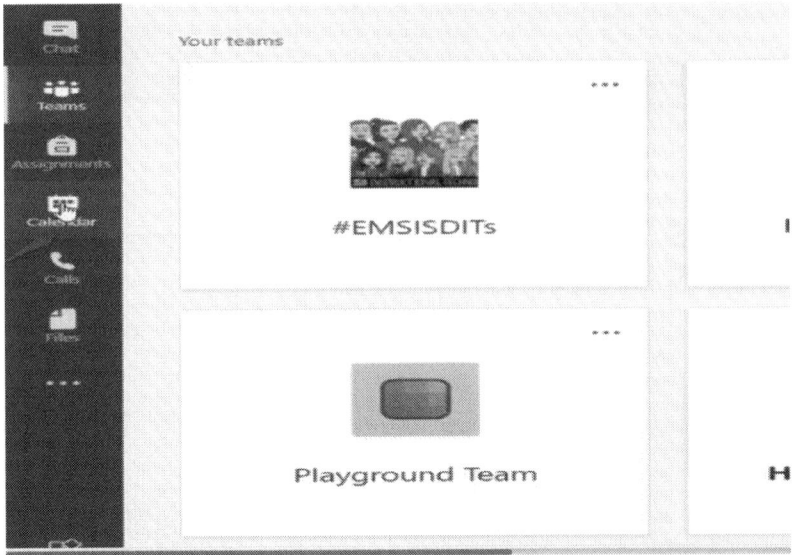

- Click on the new meeting at the top right of the Team app

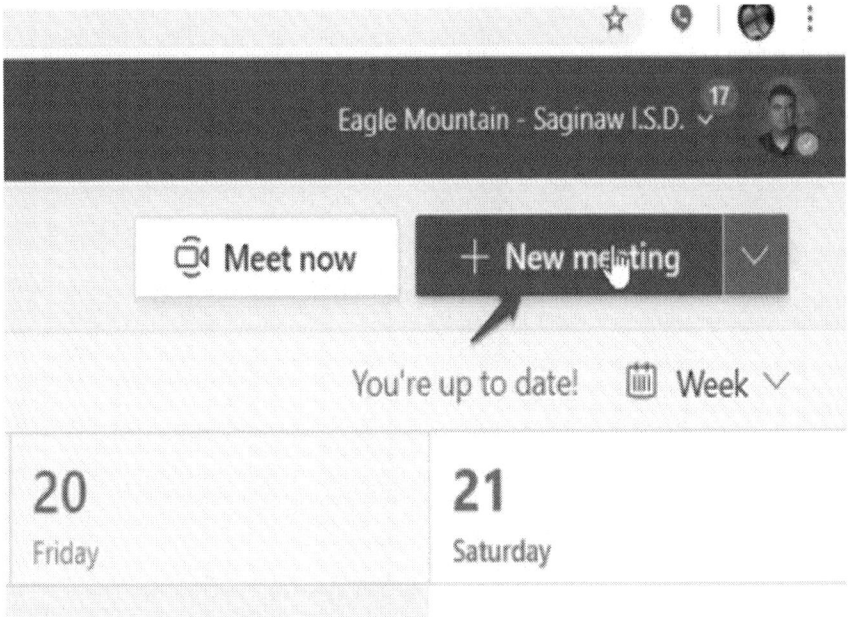

- On the next page that pops up, you will be required to give your meeting a title, add your invitees, set the time, add channel and location and the description of the new meeting.

- After the above instructions, then click on send

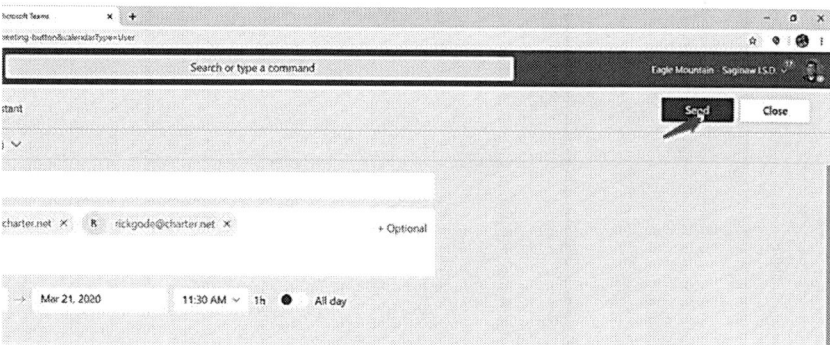

With the information above, you can definitely schedule a meeting using on Microsoft Teams.

CHAPTER THREE

BASIC TIPS AND TRICKS ON MICROSOFT TEAMS

As you get more accustomed to the use of Microsoft Team, you will be beginning to explore new tricks and tips that make the use of Microsoft Teams more interesting and adventurous. Not only that, it will definitely save you the stress of having to go through long process to get some operations carried out. In this chapter, we will be unveiling some of these tips and techniques to you. Just sit back with a cup of coffee on your table as we journey into this chapter

Command Bar and Quick Command

Command bar

The command bar is the same with the search bar and it is located at the top screen of the Microsoft Team application. This is where the Quick commands are carried out on the Microsoft Team App.

See the image below to know what a command bar is

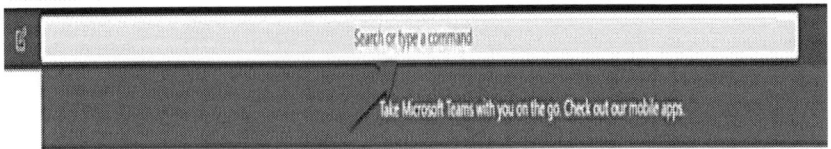

Quick command

Quick commands are shortcuts that perform an action on the Microsoft Team and they start with / or @ symbols.

Quick command @

These are commands used to search within a context. With this command, you can locate list of user and apps that are available in your Microsoft Teams.

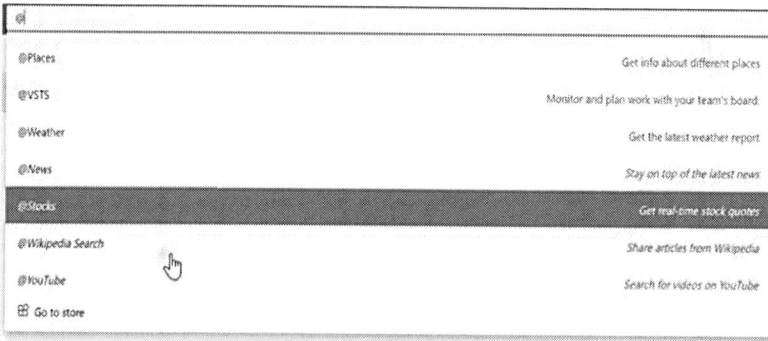

In the illustration above, you can see what pops up when you type @, these are the things you are likely to find; @places, @VST, @weather, @News, Stocks, @Wikipedia, @YouTube etc.

Commands /

These commands or shortcuts helps to quickly carry out some tasks when inputted in the task bar. Here I will be listing some / commands and their functions. Also I will be displaying few on the pages to see how they look like.

- o /activity: View a team member's activity
- o /available: Changes your Team's status to Available
- o /away: Changes your Team's status to Away
- o /busy: Changes your Team's status to Busy
- o /call: Make a call
- o /dnd: Changes your Team's status to Do Not Disturb
- o /files: See your all recent files
- o /goto: Go to a certain team or channel
- o /help: Get help (with Teams; not the "lie on the couch" kind)
- o /join: Join a team
- o /keys: View keyboard shortcuts
- o /mentions: See all of your mentions
- o /org: View an org chart (yours or someone else's)
- o /saved: View your saved list
- o /unread: See all of your unread activity
- o /what new: Check out what's new in Teams
- o /who: Ask Who (a new app that lets you search for people by name or topic) a question

Let's quickly display few of the /commands to see how they look like

How to Activate Do Not Disturb mode (dnd) on your status

Let's assume you are in the middle of a meeting and you don't want anyone to disturb, all you have to do is

- Click on the search or command box and type /dnd and press enter

  Note: Any call that comes in during the do not disturb mode will be sent directly to voicemail.

  See the illustrations below

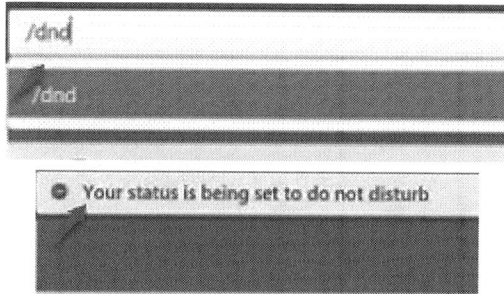

How to Locate a Channel in your Microsoft Teams

Type /goto with the name of the channel on the search or command box e.g /pipeline and click on enter

See the images below

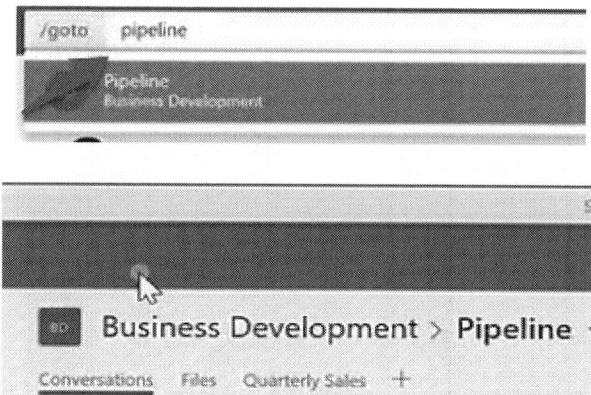

How to get Information of Anyone on your Microsoft Team Chat List

Type /who with name of the person and click enter and the next page will display all information Microsoft Teams have on the person.

See the images below

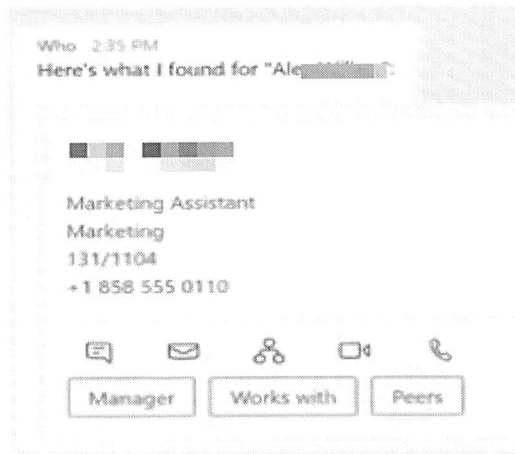

To place a call

Type /call with the name of the person you intend to call on the search or command box and click on enter

See the pictures below

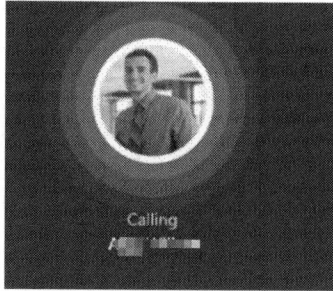

Calling

Locating any application installed on the Microsoft Team

Type @ on the search or command box and press enter

Note; This shows the list of apps in the Microsoft team

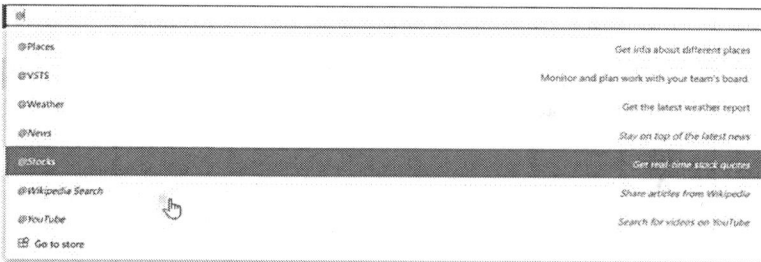

Keyboard Shortcuts

Just like / and@ commands, these shortcuts are also used to quickly carry out a task. With the image below, you can try practicing the shortcuts with your Microsoft Team app, trust me, these shortcuts will definitely come in handy.

Keyboard shortcuts ⊗

Keyboard language is: English (United States)

General

Show keyboard shortcuts	Ctrl .	Go to Search		Ctrl E
Show commands	Ctrl /	Goto		Ctrl Shift G
Start new chat	Alt N	Open Settings		Ctrl Shift ,
Open Help	Ctrl F1	Close		Escape

Navigation

Open Activity	Ctrl Shift 1	Open Chat		Ctrl Shift 2
Open Teams	Ctrl Shift 3	Open Calendar		Ctrl Shift 4
Open Files	Ctrl Shift 5	Go to previous list item		Alt ↑
Go to next list item	Alt ↓	Go to previous section		Ctrl Shift F6
Go to next section	Ctrl F6			

Messaging

Go to compose box	C	Expand compose box		Ctrl Shift X
Send (expanded compose box)	Ctrl Enter	Attach file		Ctrl Shift O
Start new line	Shift Enter	Reply to thread		R

Meetings and Calls

Accept video call	Ctrl Shift A	Accept audio call		Ctrl Shift S
Decline call	Ctrl Shift D	Start audio call		Ctrl Shift C
Start video call	Ctrl Shift U	Toggle mute		Ctrl Shift M
Go to sharing toolbar	Ctrl Shift Space			

See shortcuts for all platforms   Office Accessibility Centre

CHAPTER FOUR

COMMON ERRORS IN MICROSOFT TEAMS AND HOW THEY CAN BE FIXED

Without doubts, it is clear that Microsoft teams is not just a very good application, but also a very useful and wonderful application especially to those in the business world. However, there are certain problems that can make the use of Microsoft teams very frustrating and some of these reasons are what we will be talking about in this chapter so that when you come across them, they wouldn't appear strange to you.

How to Recover Lost Password

In case you must have forgotten your Microsoft accounts password, do not fret; Microsoft Teams has got you covered! Just follow the steps below to get it recovered.

- Open the Microsoft account, enter your email address and click next

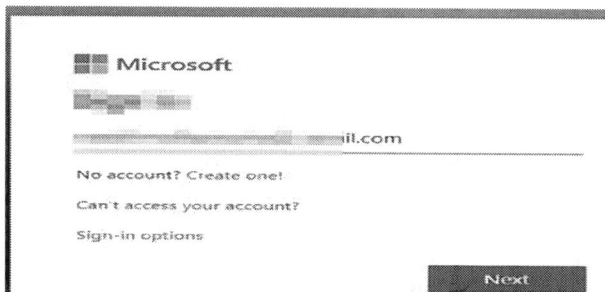

- Click forget password

Microsoft

████████████████████.com

████████████████

Password
_____

☐ Keep me signed in

Forgot password?

- In the next page, you will be asked if you wish to get the code via the email inputted then click get code

Microsoft

We need to verify your identity

How would you like to get your security code?

◉ E██████████████████████nail.com

I have a code

I don't have any of these

Cancel	Get code

- Enter the code sent and press next

Microsoft

Verify your identity

com. Check your email
for a ccount team, and
enter

Enter code

Use a different verification option

Cancel   Next

- In this page, type the password you intend to change
  and re-enter again then click on next

Reset your password

8-character minimum; case sensitive

New password

Reenter password

Cancel   Next

- In this page, your password will be changed then you can click on sign in

Summary of what you've completed:

Your password was changed

Sign in

How to Unlock Microsoft Account

- Click next on the displayed account

Your account has been locked

We've detected some activity that violates our Microsoft Services Agreement and have locked your account.

Unlocking your account

...ode to ...an get back into your account.

Next

- In this page, you will be instructed to input your number and after this, click on send code

we'll send you a security code

We'll send a verification code in a text message. This helps us eliminate spam – we won't give out your number. The code will expire in about 10 minutes.

Country code

India (+91)   ▼

Send code

- In this page, type in the access code sent and enter submit

I didn't get a code

Enter the access code

8881

Why do I have to do this?

Submit

- In this page, account unlocked will be displayed so you can click on continue to log in

Microsoft

Your account has been unblocked

If you believe someone else might have accessed your account, please review your Recent Activity.

For tips on how to make your Microsoft account more secure, click here.

Continue

How to Fix "File Upload Failed" Error In Microsoft Teams

This occurs when the One drive is full and to get this fixed up, follow the steps below:

- Open One drive with the same account you are using for Microsoft teams

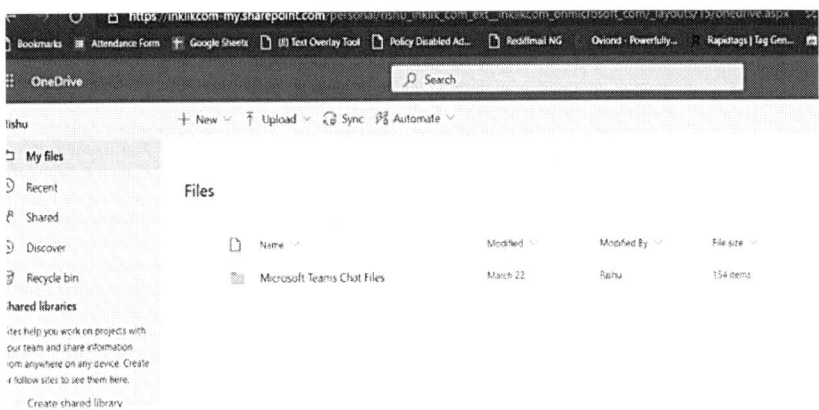

- In this page, you will see a file called Microsoft chat file, click on it

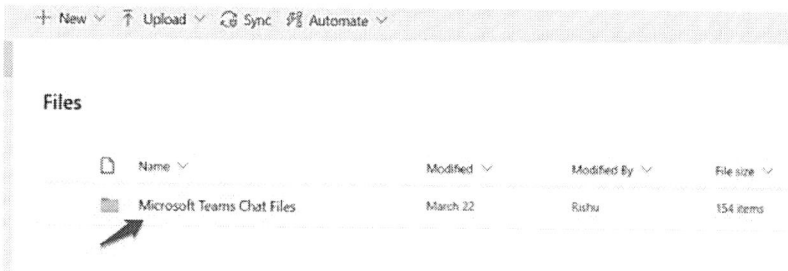

- Select the files you no longer need

- Click on delete

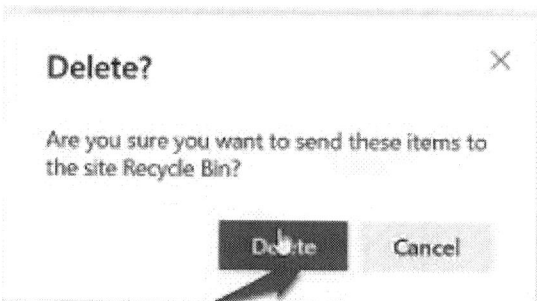

- Go to the recycle bin and delete the files

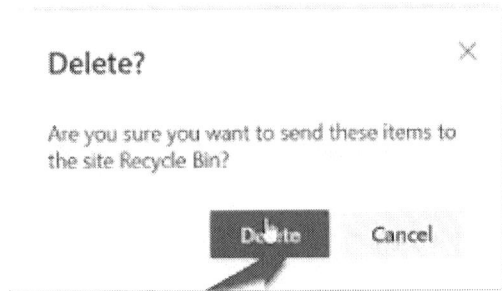

- Open your Microsoft Teams and send the file again

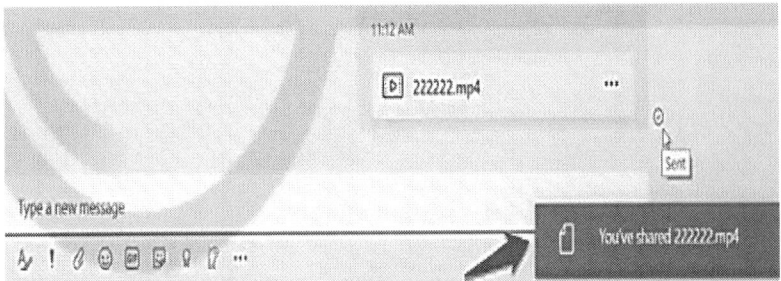

How to Fix Microphone in Microsoft Teams

- Open the Microsoft Team and click on the profile account

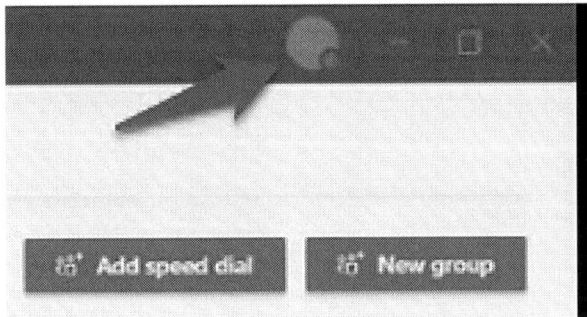

- Click on the setting

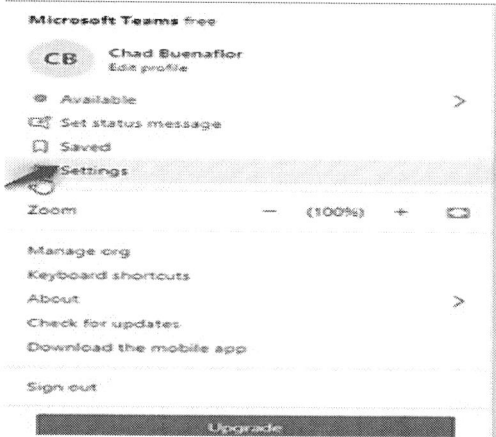

- Click on devices

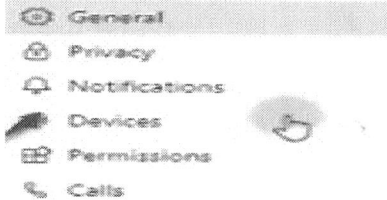

- Select microphone and click on any of your choice

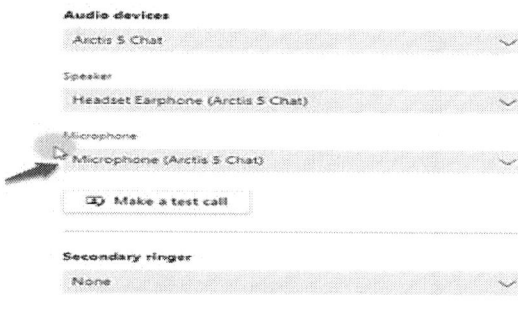

- Then allow apps to access the microphone

How to Allow Apps Access the Microphone

To get this done, follow the steps below:

- Go to start button and click on settings

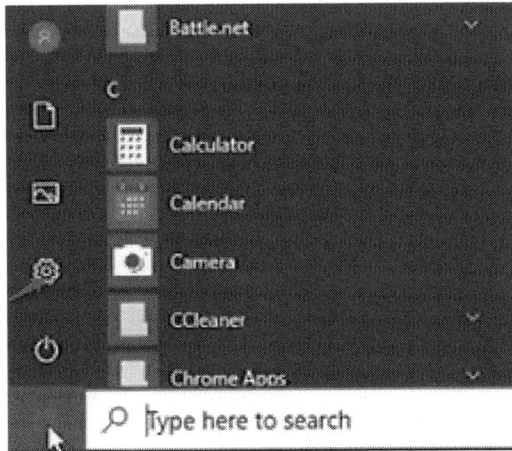

- Click on Privacy

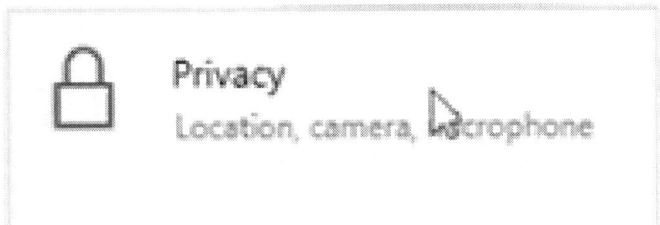

- Click on the microphone and allow the apps notification settings for microphone

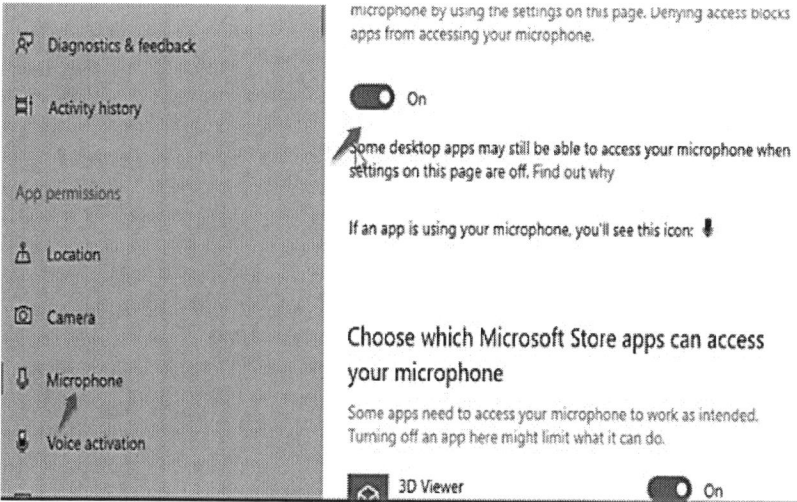

microphone by using the settings on this page. Denying access blocks apps from accessing your microphone.

On

Some desktop apps may still be able to access your microphone when settings on this page are off. Find out why

If an app is using your microphone, you'll see this icon: 🎤

Choose which Microsoft Store apps can access your microphone

Some apps need to access your microphone to work as intended. Turning off an app here might limit what it can do.

3D Viewer   **On**

- Then run the recording audio troubleshooting

How to Run the Recording Audio Troubleshooting

- Go to the start button and click on settings

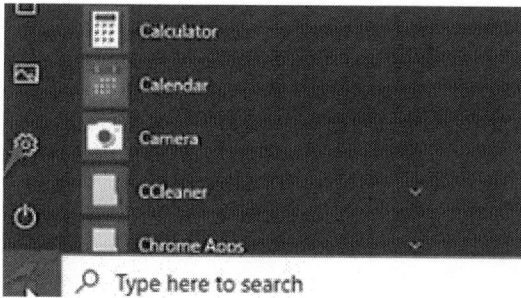

- Go to update and security

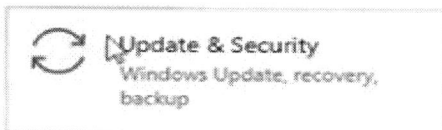

Update & Security
Windows Update, recovery, backup

- Click on troubleshoot

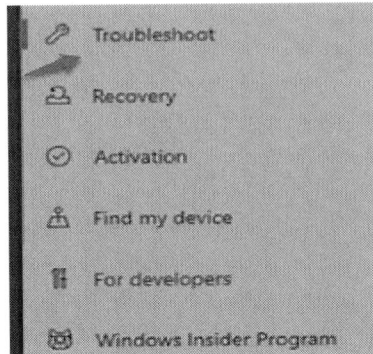

- Locate the recording audio and start the trouble shooting

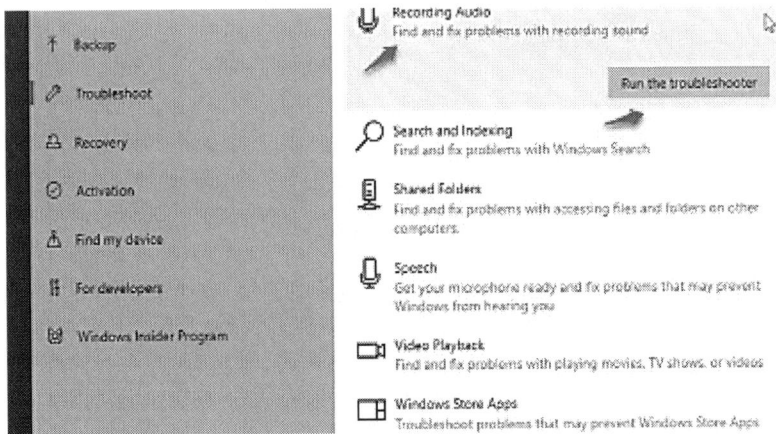

- Then follow the on screen instructions

How to Fix Camera in Microsoft Teams

- Open Microsoft Teams and click on the profile account

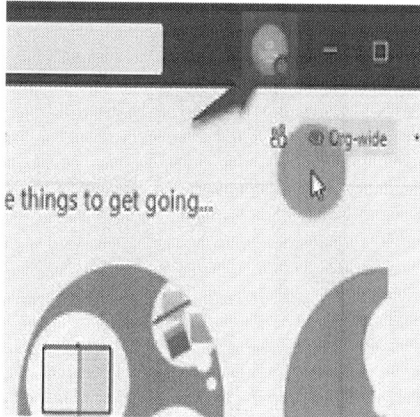

- Go to settings

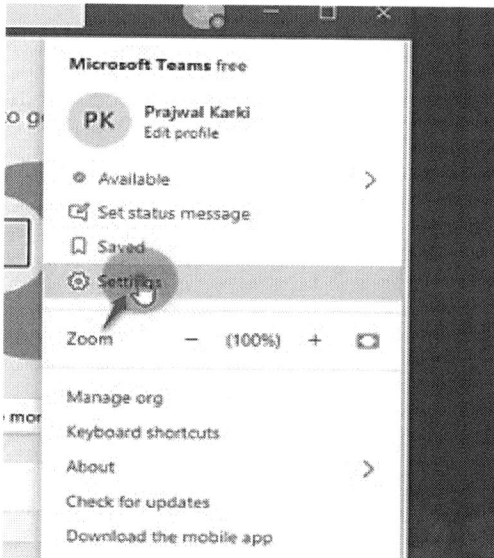

- Then click on devices to check the camera

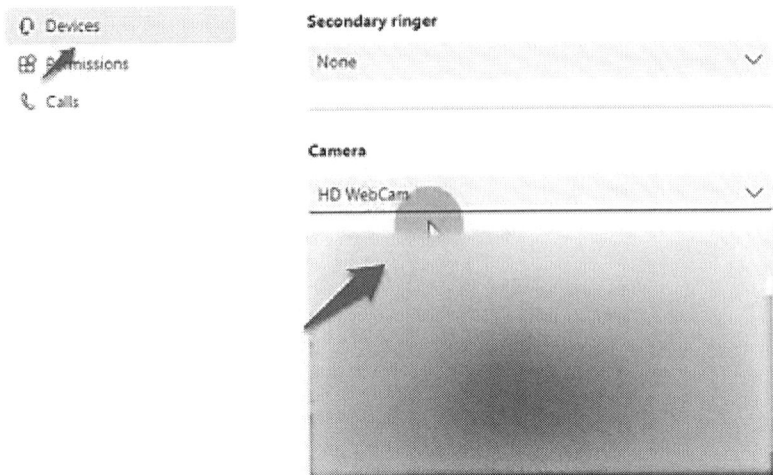

- Go the start button, search for camera and click on it

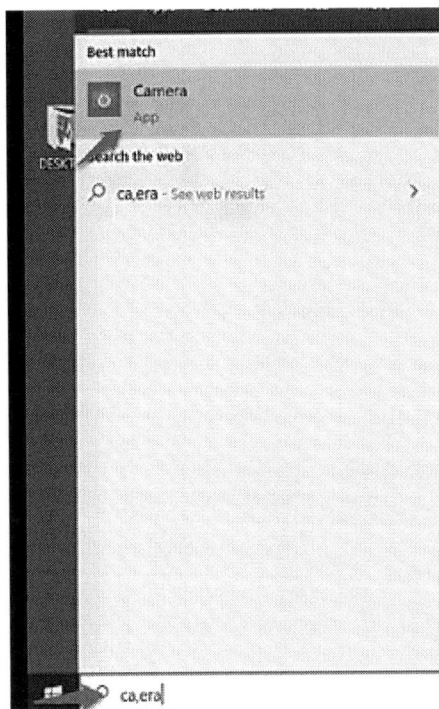

- When this page pops up click on privacy settings

We need your permission

To use this app, open Privacy settings, and change the settings to allow this app to use your camera and microphone.

| Privacy settings | Get help | OK |

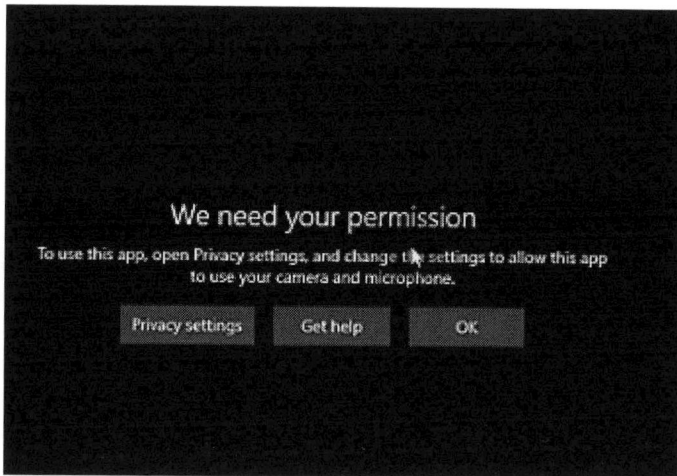

- Then go to allow all apps to access camera and hit the yes button

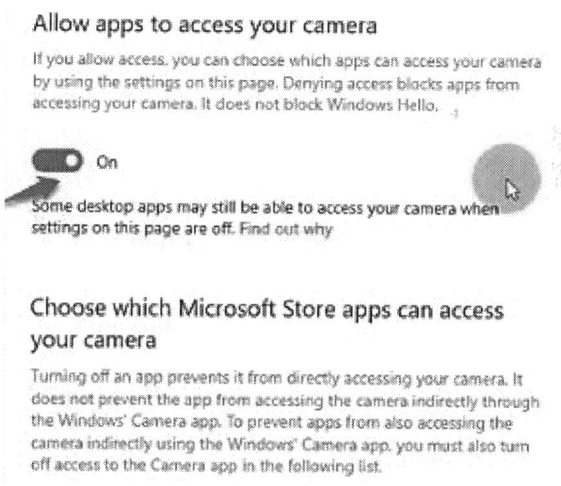

Allow apps to access your camera

If you allow access, you can choose which apps can access your camera by using the settings on this page. Denying access blocks apps from accessing your camera. It does not block Windows Hello.

On

Some desktop apps may still be able to access your camera when settings on this page are off. Find out why

Choose which Microsoft Store apps can access your camera

Turning off an app prevents it from directly accessing your camera. It does not prevent the app from accessing the camera indirectly through the Windows' Camera app. To prevent apps from also accessing the camera indirectly using the Windows' Camera app, you must also turn off access to the Camera app in the following list.

- Close settings to see the camera working

CONCLUSION

In this time and season with the way technology is advancing, Microsoft teams is one of those leading applications that business organizations or enterprises must not joke with.

With the features embedded in Microsoft Teams, it is highly recommended that organizations in the world at large should start getting accustomed to it.

Not only is Microsoft Teams useful in the business world, it is very relevant in educational sectors.

As a business man, you can interact with your clients anytime anywhere.

As a student, the acquisition of knowledge is no longer difficult to get. You can keep in touch with your colleagues as well your teachers.

With Microsoft Teams, life is made easier!

About The Author

My name is James Jordan, I am an author who is passionate about my customers' satisfaction and always puts my customers' needs at the front line. I am a content writer and a publisher who drives passion in providing solutions to people in online businesses.

Follow my author page for updates on my other books.
One of the things that makes an author do more is getting customers' feedback and reviews.
Kindly leave a feedback after reading this book.
I will really appreciate it.

James Jordan

Made in the USA
Monee, IL
22 September 2020